~ To Laura

You are special to us all!

Love,

Lauren, Renny, & LeAnn

A LITTLE
TREASURY
OF GOLD

POEMS OF LOVE AND FAITH

COMPILED BY
KAY ANNE CARSON

INSPIRATIONAL PRESS
NEW YORK

FOR BILL WITH LOVE AND FAITH

Published in 1993 by
INSPIRATIONAL PRESS
A division of Budget Book Service, Inc.
386 Park Avenue South
Suite 1913
New York, NY 10016

Inspirational Press is a registered trademark of
Budget Book Service, Inc.

Library of Congress Catalog Card Number: 92-70345
ISBN: 0-88486-062-0

Designed by Cindy LaBreacht.
Printed in Hong Kong.

ACKNOWLEDGEMENTS

Sincere thanks are due the following publishers
for cooperation in allowing the use of poems selected from
their publications:

Charles Scribner's & Sons for selections from
"Be Strong" by Maltbie D. Babcock.

Funk & Wagnalls Company for "Life and Death"
from *Swords and Plowshares* by Ernest Crosby.

Hope Publishing Company for "Thy Will Be Done
in Me" from *Bells at Evening* by Fanny Crosby.

Houghton, Mifflin Company for poems by Whittier,
Lowell, and Harriet Beecher Stowe.

Macmillan Publishing Company and A.P. Watt Limited
on behalf of Michael B. Yeats and Macmillan London
Ltd. for "When You Are Old" from *The Poems of W.B.
Yeats: A New Edition*, edited by Richard J. Finneran.
Copyright 1928 by Macmillan Publishing Company,
renewed 1956 by Georgie Yeats

W.B. Conkey & Company for "A Morning Prayer,"
from *Poems of Power* by Ella Wheeler Wilcox.

CONTENTS

ANCHORED TO THE INFINITE

The builder who first bridged Niagara's gorge,
  Before he swung his cable, shore to shore,
  Sent out across the gulf his venturing kite
  Bearing a slender cord for unseen hands
    To grasp upon a further cliff and draw
    A greater cord, and then a greater yet;
      Till at last across the chasm swung
    The cable—then the mighty bridge in air!

  So we may send our little timid thought
  Across the void, out to God's reaching hands
  Send out our love and faith to thread the deep,
    Thought after thought until the little cord
  Has greatened to a chain no chance can break,
      And—we are anchored to the Infinite!

EDWIN MARKHAM

I.

look
to this
day

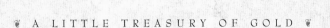

LOOK TO THIS DAY

Look to this day!
For it is life, the very life of life.
In its brief course lie all the varieties and realities
of your existence:
The bliss of growth;
The glory of action;
The splendor of beauty;
For yesterday is already a dream, and tomorrow
is only a vision;
But today, well lived, makes every yesterday
A dream of happiness, and every tomorrow a
vision of hope.
Look well, therefore, to this day!
Such is the salutation of the dawn!

FROM THE SANSKRIT

BE STRONG!

Be strong!
We are not here to play, to dream, to drift,
We have hard work to do, and loads to lift.
Shun not the struggle, face it, 'tis God's gift.

Be strong!
Say not the days are evil—who's to blame!
And fold the hands and acquiesce—O shame!
Stand up, speak out, and bravely, in God's name.

Be strong!
It matters not how deep entrenched the wrong,
How hard the battle goes, the day, how long;
Faint not, fight on! To-morrow comes the song.

MALTBIE D. BABCOCK

THE RAINY DAY

The day is cold and dark and dreary;
It rains, and the wind is never weary;
The vine still clings to the moldering wall,
But at every gust the dead leaves fall,
And the day is dark and dreary.

My life is cold and dark and dreary;
It rains, and the wind is never weary;
My thoughts still cling to the moldering past,
But the hopes of youth fall thick in the blast,
And the days are dark and dreary.

Be still, sad heart! and cease repining;
Behind the clouds is the sun still shining:
Thy fate is the common fate of all:
Into each life some rain must fall,
Some days must be dark and dreary.

HENRY W. LONGFELLOW

HOW DID HE LIVE?

So he died for his faith. That is fine.
More than most of us do.
But stay. Can you add to that line
That he lived for it, too?

It is easy to die. Men have died
For a wish or a whim—
From bravado or passion or pride.
Was it harder for him?

But to live; every day to live out
All the truth that he dreamt,
While his friends met his conduct with doubt,
And the world with contempt.

Was it thus that he plodded ahead,
Never turning aside?
Then we'll talk of the life that he led.
Never mind how he died.

ERNEST CROSBY

I WOULD BE GREAT

O Lord,
I would be great—
But not in some spectacular way
For world acclaim.
Beyond my talents
Lie outstanding deeds, perhaps;
But, Lord, I would be great
In faithfulness to each small task
Thou givest me,
To do the best I can
With what I have
For Thy name's sake.

And if, some day, Thou sendest me
Some task that seems too big
For hands that only little deeds have done,
I know that what I cannot do,
Thou canst, through me, if I but will,
And in Thy strength
I'll do the thing that is too big for me.
Help me, O Lord, to stand approved
In faithfulness to every task.
Thus, in Thy sight
I will be great.

HATTIE B. McCRACKEN

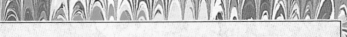

PIPPA'S SONG

The year's at the spring,
The day's at the morn;
Morning's at seven:
The hillside's dew pearled;
The lark's on the wing;
The snail's on the thorn;
God's in His heaven—
All's right with the world!

ROBERT BROWNING
FROM "PIPPA PASSES"

THE COMMON PROBLEM

The common problem—yours, mine,
everyone's—
Is not to fancy what were fair in life
Provided it could be; but, finding first
What may be, then find how to make it fair
Up to our means—a very different thing?
My business is not to remake myself
But make the absolute best of what God made.

ROBERT BROWNING

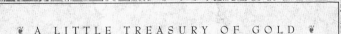

A MORNING PRAYER

Let me today do something that will take
A little sadness from the world's vast store,
And my I be so favored as to make
Of joy's too scanty sum a little more.

Let me not hurt, by any selfish deed
Or thoughtless word, the heart of foe or friend.
Nor would I pass unseeing worthy need,
Or sin by silence when I should defend.

However meager be my worldly wealth,
Let me give something that shall aid my kind—
A word of courage, or a thought of health
Dropped as I pass for troubled hearts to find.

Let me tonight look back across the span
'Twixt dawn and dark, and to my conscience say—
Because of some good act to beast or man—
"The world is better that I lived today."

ELLA WHEELER WILCOX

A POET LIVED IN GALILEE

A Poet lived in Galilee,
Whose mother dearly knew him,
And his beauty like a cooling tree
Drew many people to him.

He had sweet-hearted things to say,
And he was angry only
When people were unkind. That day
He'd stand there straight and lonely.

And tell them what they ought to do:
"Love other folks," he pleaded,
"As you love me and I love you;"
Yet almost no one heeded.

A Poet lived in Galilee,
They stared at him and slew him.
What would they do to you and me
If we could say we knew him?

WITTER BYNNER

II.

each
man is
captain
of his
soul

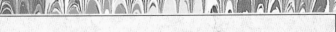

WE BREAK NEW SEAS TODAY

Each man is Captain of his Soul,
And each man his own Crew,
But the Pilot knows the Unknown Seas,
And he will bring us through.

We break new seas today—
Our eager keels quest unaccustomed waters,
And, from the vast uncharted waste in front,
The mystic circles leap
To greet our prows with mightiest possibilities,
Bringing us—What?

Dread shoals and shifting banks?
And calms and storms?
And clouds and biting gales?
And wreck and loss?
And valiant fighting times?
And, maybe, death?—and so, the Larger Life!

For, should the Pilot deem it best
To cut the voyage short,
He sees beyond the sky-line, and
He'll bring us into Port!

JOHN OXENHAM

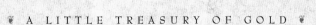

ST. FRANCIS' PRAYER

Lord, make me an instrument of Thy peace.
Where there is hate, may I bring love;
Where offense, may I bring pardon;
May I bring union in place of discord;
Truth, replacing error;
Faith, where once there was doubt;
Hope, for despair;
Light, where was darkness;
Joy to replace sadness.
Make me not to so crave to be loved as to love.
Help me to learn that in giving I may receive;
In forgetting self, I may find life eternal.

ST. FRANCIS OF ASSISI

THY WILL BE DONE IN ME

O Thou to whom, without reserve,
My all I would resign,
I ask for grace and faith to say,
"Thy will, O Lord, not mine!"
In joy or grief, in bliss or pain,
This prayer shall rise to Thee,
"Thy will, not mine, O blessed Lord,
Thy will be done in me!"

Though thorns may pierce my weary feet,
Yet would I ne'er repine,
But meekly say, as Thou hast said,
"thy will, O Lord, not mine!"
And though I pass beneath Thy rod,
Amen, so let it be!
Whate'er Thou wilt, O blessed Lord,
I know is best for me.

So would I live that I may feel
Thy perfect peace divine,
And still Thy pure example show
In every act of mine;
And till I reach the silent vale,
and cross the narrow sea,
Be this my prayer, O blessed Lord,
"Thy will be done in me!"

FANNY CROSBY

BETRAYAL

Still as of old
Men by themselves are priced—
For thirty pieces Judas sold
Himself, not Christ.

HESTER H. CHOLMONDELEY

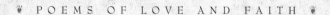

I WOULD BE TRUE

I would be true, for there are those who trust me;
I would be pure, for there are those who care;
I would be strong, for there is much to suffer;
I would be brave, for there is much to dare.

I would be friend of all—the foe, the friendless;
I would be giving, and forget the gift;
I would be humble, for I know my weakness;
I would look up, and laugh, and love, and lift.

I would be learning, day by day, the lessons
My heavenly Father gives me in his Word;
I would be quick to hear his lightest whisper,
And prompt and glad to do the things I've heard.

HOWARD ARNOLD WALTER

WHICHEVER WAY THE WIND
DOTH BLOW

Whichever way the wind doth blow
Some heart is glad to have it so;
Then blow it east or blow it west,
The wind that blows, that wind is best.

My little craft sails not alone;
A thousand fleets from every zone
Are out upon a thousand seas;
And what for me were favouring breeze
Might dash another, with the shock
Of doom, upon some hidden rock.
And so I do not dare to pray
For winds to waft me on my way,

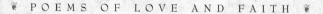

But leave it to a Higher Will
To stay or speed me; trusting still
That all is well, and sure that He
Who launched my bark will sail with me
Through storm and calm, and will not fail
Whatever breezes may prevail
To land me, every peril past,
Within His sheltering Heaven at last.

Then whatsoever wind doth blow,
My heart is glad to have it so;
And blow it east or blow it west,
The wind that blows, that wind is best.

CAROLINE ATHERTON MASON

III.

the star
to every
wandering
bark

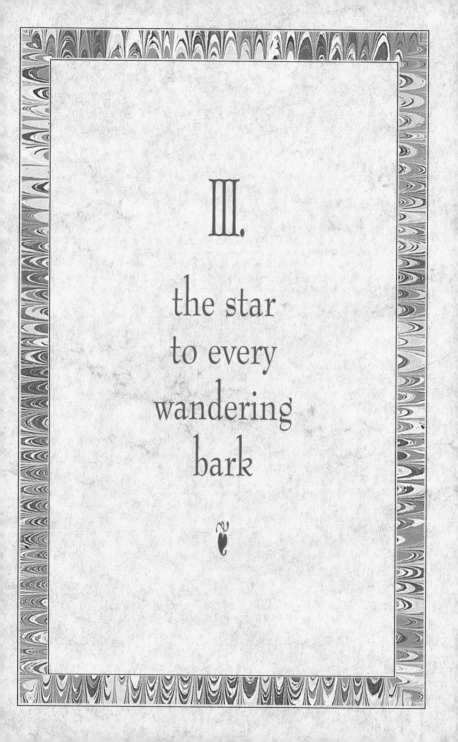

TRUE LOVE

Let me not to the marriage of true minds
Admit impediments. Love is not love
Which alters when it alteration finds,
Or bends with the remover to remove.
O, no! it is an ever-fixèd mark,
That looks on tempests and is never shaken;
It is the star to every wandering bark,
Whose worth's unknown, although his height
be taken.

Love's not Time's fool, though rosy lips and
cheeks
Within his bending sickle's compass come;
Love alters not with his brief hours and weeks,
But bears it out even to the edge of doom.
If this be error and upon me proved,
I never writ, nor no man ever loved.

WILLIAM SHAKESPEARE

UPON THE SAND

All love that has not friendship for its base,
Is like a mansion built upon the sand.
Though brave its walls as any in the land,
And its tall turrets lift their heads in grace;
Though skillful and accomplished artists trace
Most beautiful designs on every hand,
And gleaming statues in dim niches stand,
And fountains play in some flow'r-hidden place:

Yet, when from the frowning east a sudden gust
Of adverse fate is blown, or sad rains fall
Day in, day out, against its yielding wall,
Lo! the fair structure crumbles to the dust.
Love, to endure life's sorrow and earth's woe,
Needs friendship's solid masonwork below.

ELLA WHEELER WILCOX

LOVE

I love you,
Not only for what you are,
But for what I am
When I am with you.

I love you,
Not only for what
You have made of yourself,
But for what
You are making of me.

I love you
For the part of me
That you bring out;
I love you
For putting your hand
Into my heaped-up heart
And passing over
All the foolish, weak things

That you can't help
Dimly seeing there,
And for drawing out
Into the light
All the beautiful belongings
That no one else had looked
Quite far enough to find.

I love you because you
Are helping me to make
Of the lumber of my life
Not a tavern
But a temple;
Out of the works
Of my every day
Not a reproach
But a song . . .

AUTHOR UNKNOWN

MARRIAGE

I know we loved each other when we walked
So long ago in spring beneath the moon;
When, hand clasped close in hand, we softly talked
Of that new joy our hearts would shelter soon,
Perennially golden and secure
From any change. But O, we could not see
That springtime wonderment would not endure
As first it was but alter blessedly.
We could not know, my dear, we could not guess
How years augment the miracle of love;
How autumn brings a depth of tenderness
That is beyond young April's dreaming of!
How there would burn a richer flame some day
Than that which first threw glory on our way.

A. WARREN

TRUE LOVE

True love is but a humble, low-born thing,
And hath its food served up in earthenware;
It is a thing to walk with, hand in hand,
Through the everydayness of this work-day
world,
Baring its tender feet to every roughness,
Yet letting not one heart-beat go astray
From beauty's law of plainness and content—
A simple, fireside thing, whose quiet smile
Can warm earth's poorest hovel to a home.

JAMES RUSSELL LOWELL

THE NEWLY-WEDDED

Now the rite is duly done,
Now the word is spoken,
And the spell has made us one
Which may ne'er be broken;
Rest we, dearest, in our home,
Roam we o'er the heather:
We shall rest, and we shall roam
Shall we not? together.

From this hour the summer rose
Sweeter breathes to charm us;
From this hour the winter snows
Lighter fall to harm us:

Fair or foul—on land or sea—
Come the wind or weather,
Best and worst, whate'er they be,
We shall share together.

Death, who friend from friend can part,
Brother rend from brother,
Shall but link us, heart and heart,
Closer to each other:
We will call his anger play,
Deem his dart a feather,
When we meet him on our way
Hand in hand together.

WINTHROP MACKWORTH PRAED

THE DAY IS DONE

The day is done, and the darkness
Falls from the wings of Night,
As a feather is wafted downward
From an eagle in his flight.

I see the lights of the village
Gleam through the rain and the mist,
And a feeling of sadness comes o'er me
That my soul cannot resist.

A feeling of sadness and longing,
That is not akin to pain,
And resembles sorrow only
As the mist resembles the rain.

Come, read to me some poem,
Some simple and heartfelt lay,
That shall soothe this restless feeling,
And banish the thoughts of day.

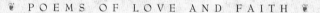

POEMS OF LOVE AND FAITH

Such songs have power to quiet
The restless pulse of care,
And come like the benediction
That follows after prayer.

Then read from the treasured volume
The poem of thy choice,
And lend to the rhyme of the poet
The beauty of thy voice.

And the night shall be filled with music,
And the cares, that infest the day,
Shall fold their tents, like the Arabs,
And as silently steal away.

HENRY WADSWORTH LONGFELLOW

33

NOT OURS THE VOWS

Not ours the vows of such as plight
Their troth in sunny weather,
While leaves are green, and skies are bright
To walk on flowers together.

But we have loved as those who tread
The thorny path of sorrow,
With clouds above, and cause to dread
Yet deeper gloom tomorrow.

That thorny path, those stormy skies,
Have drawn our spirits nearer;
And rendered us, by sorrow's ties,
Each to the other dearer.

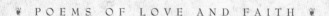

Love, born in hours of joy and mirth,
With mirth and joy may perish;
That to which darker hours gave birth,
Still more and more we cherish.

It looks beyond the clouds of time,
And through death's shadowy portal;
Made by adversity sublime,
By faith and hope immortal.

BERNARD BARTON

PRAYER OF ANY HUSBAND

Lord, may there be no moment in her life
When she regrets that she became my wife,
And keep her dear eyes just a trifle blind
To my defects, and to my failings kind!

Help me to do the utmost that I can
To prove myself her measure of a man,
But, if I often fail as mortals may,
Grant that she never sees my feet of clay!
And let her make allowance—now and then—
That we are only grown-up boys, we men,
So, loving all our children, she will see,
Sometimes, a remnant of the child in me!

Since years must bring to all their load of care,
Let us together every burden bear,
And when Death beckons one its path along,
May not the two of us be parted long!

MAZIE V. CARUTHERS

LOVE IS OF GOD

Beloved, let us love: love is of God;
In God alone hath love its true abode.

Beloved, let us love: for they who love,
They only, are His sons, born from above.

Beloved, let us love: for love is rest,
And he who loveth not abides unblest.

Beloved, let us love: for love is light,
And he who loveth not dwelleth in night.

Beloved, let us love: for only thus
Shall we behold that God Who loveth us.

HORATIUS BONAR

IV.

better
than grandeur
better
than gold

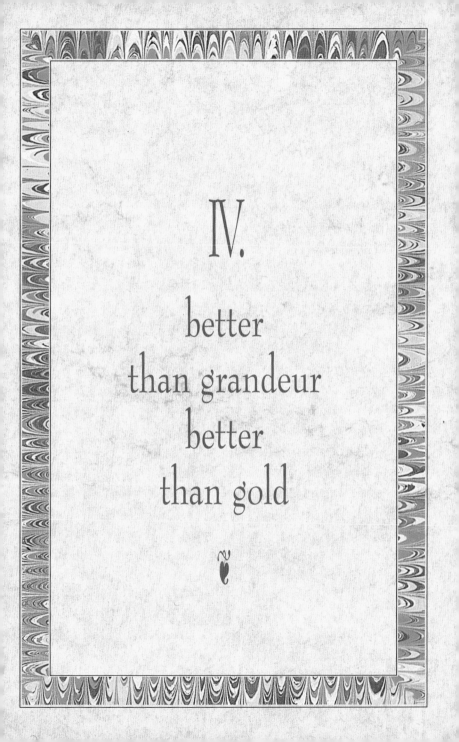

BETTER THAN GOLD

Better than grandeur, better than gold,
Than rank and titles a thousandfold,
Is a healthy body and mind at ease,
And simple pleasures that always please.

A heart that can feel for another's woe,
And share his joys with a genial glow;
With sympathies large enough to enfold
All men as brothers, is better than gold.

Better than gold is a conscience clear,
Though toiling for bread in an humble sphere,
Doubly blessed with content and health,
Untried by the lusts and cares of wealth,

Lowly living and lofty thought
Adorn and ennoble a poor man's cot;
For mind and morals in nature's plan
Are the genuine tests of an earnest man.

Better than gold is a peaceful home
Where all the fireside characters come,
The shrine of love, the heaven of life,
Hallowed by mother, or sister, or wife.
However humble the home may be,
Or tried with sorrow by heaven's decree,
The blessings that never were bought or sold,
And center there, are better than gold.

ABRAM J. RYAN

HOME, SWEET HOME!

Mid pleasures and palaces though we may roam,
Be it ever so humble, there's no place like home;
A charm from the sky seems to hallow us there,
Which, seek through the world, is ne'er met with
elsewhere.
Home, Home, sweet, sweet Home!
There's no place like Home! there's no place
like Home!

An exile from home, splendour dazzles in vain;
O, give me my lowly thatched cottage again!
The birds singing gayly, that came at my call,—
Give me them, —and the peace of mind, dearer
than all!
Home, Home, sweet, sweet Home!
There's no place like Home! there's no place
like Home!

How sweet 't is to sit 'neath a fond father's
smile,
And the cares of a mother to soothe and beguile!
Let others delight mid new pleasures to roam,
But give me, oh, give me, the pleasures of home!
Home! Home! sweet, sweet Home!
There's no place like Home! there's no place
like Home!

To thee I'll return, overburdened with care;
The heart's dearest solace will smile on me there;
No more from that cottage again will I roam;
Be it ever so humble, there's no place like home.
Home! Home! sweet, sweet Home!
There's no place like Home! there's no place
like Home!

JOHN HOWARD PAYNE

THE GREATEST WORK

He built a house; time laid it in the dust;
He wrote a book, its title now forgot;
He ruled a city, but his name is not
On any table graven, or where rust
Can gather from disuse, or marble bust.
He took a child from out a wretched cot,
Who on the state dishonor might have brought,
And reared him to the Christian's hope and trust.
The boy, to manhood grown, became a light
To many souls, and preached for human need
The wondrous love of the Omnipotent.
The work has multiplied like stars at night
When darkness deepens; every noble deed
Lasts longer than a granite monument.

AUTHOR UNKNOWN

THE MOTHER'S HYMN

Lord who ordainst for mankind
Benignant toils and tender cares,
We thank thee for the ties that bind
The mother to the child she bears.

We thank thee for the hopes that rise
Within her heart, as, day by day,
The dawning soul, from those young eyes,
Looks with a clearer, steadier ray.

And grateful for the blessing given
With that dear infant on her knee,
She trains the eye to look to heaven,
The voice to lisp a prayer to Thee.

Such thanks the blessed Mary gave
When from her lap the Holy Child,
Sent from on high to seek and save
The lost of earth, looked up and smiled.

All-Gracious! grant to those who bear
A mother's charge, the strength and light
To guide the feet that own their care
In ways of Love and Truth and Right.

WILLIAM CULLEN BRYANT

THE BIBLE

We search the world for truth. We cull
The good, the true, the beautiful,
From graven stone and written scroll,
And all old flower-fields of the soul;
And, weary seekers of the best,
We come back laden from our quest,
To find that all the sages said
Is in the Book our mothers read.

JOHN GREENLEAF WHITTIER

A VOICE

The Father too, does He not see and hear?
And seems He far who dwells so very near?
Fear not, my child, there is no need to fear.

The days may darken and the tempest lower;
Their power is nothing to the Father's power;
Lift up thy heart and watch with me this hour.

The Shepherd loves and seeks the straying sheep;
Them that are His He must forever keep;
Oh dry thine eyes, there is no need to weep.

Though night falls round Him and cold rains are
blown,
And bleak the hills, He searches still alone,
And search He must until He find His own.

SAMUEL VALENTINE COLE

THE BLIND CHILD

I know what mother's face is like,
Although I cannot see;
It's like the music of a bell;
It's like the roses I can smell—
Yes, these it's like to me.

I know what father's face is like;
I'm sure I know it all;
It's like his whistle on the air;
It's like his arms which take such care
And never let me fall.

And I can tell what God is like—
The God whom no one sees.
He's everything my parents seem;
He's fairer than my fondest dream,
And greater than all these.

AUTHOR UNKNOWN

BUILDING A TEMPLE

A builder builded a temple,
He wrought it with grace and skill;
Pillars and groins and arches
All fashioned to work his will.

Men said, as they saw its beauty,
"It shall never know decay.
Great is thy skill, O builder:
Thy fame shall endure for aye."

A teacher builded a temple
With loving and infinite care,
Planning each arch with patience,
Laying each stone with prayer.
None praised her unceasing efforts,
None knew of her wondrous plan;
For the temple the teacher builded
Was unseen by the eyes of man.

Gone is the builder's temple,
Crumbled into the dust;
Low lies each stately pillar,
Food for consuming rust.
But the temple the teacher builded
Will last while the ages roll,
For that beautiful unseen temple
Is a child's immortal soul.

AUTHOR UNKNOWN

HOUSE AND HOME

A house is built of logs and stone,
Of tiles and posts and piers;
A home is built of loving deeds
That stand a thousand years.

VICTOR HUGO

MOTHER'S LOVE

Her love is like an island
In life's ocean, vast and wide,
A peaceful, quiet shelter
From the wind and rain, and tide.

'Tis bound on the north by Hope,
By Patience on the west,
By tender Counsel on the south,
And on the east by Rest.

Above it like a beacon light
Shine faith, and truth, and prayer;
And through the changing scenes of life,
I find a haven there.

AUTHOR UNKNOWN

FRIENDS OLD AND NEW

Make new friends, but keep the old;
Those are silver, these are gold;
New-made friendships, like new wine,
Age will mellow and refine.
Friendships that have stood the test—
Time and change—are surely best;
Brow may wrinkle, hair grow gray,
Friendship never knows decay,

For 'mid old friends, tried and true,
Once more we our youth renew.
But old friends, alas! may die,
New friends must their place supply.
Cherish friendship in your breast;
New is good, but old is best;
Make new friends, but keep the old;
Those are silver, these are gold.

AUTHOR UNKNOWN

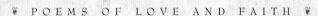

THE STIMULUS OF FRIENDSHIP

Because of your firm faith, I kept the track
Whose sharp set stones my strength had almost
spent—
I could not meet your eyes, if I turned back,
So on I went.

Because of your strong love, I held my path
When battered, worn and bleeding in the fight—
How could I meet your true eyes, blazing wrath?
So I kept right.

AUTHOR UNKNOWN

V.

beyond
the beauty
of the
now

BECAUSE YOU LOVE ME

Because you love me, I have found
New joys that were not mine before;
New stars have lightened up my sky
With glories growing more and more.
Because you love me I can rise
To the heights of fame and realms of power;
Because you love me I may learn
The highest use of every hour.

Because you love me I can choose
To look through your dear eyes and see
Beyond the beauty of the Now
Far onward to Eternity.

Because you love me I can wait
With perfect patience well possessed;
Because you love me all my life
Is circled with unquestioned rest;
Yes, even Life and even Death
Is all unquestioned and all blest.

PALL MALL MAGAZINE

SOMETHING BEYOND

Something beyond! Though now, with joy
unfounded,
The life-task falleth from thy weary hand,
Be brave, be patient! in the fair Beyond
Thou'lt understand.

Something beyond! Ah, if it were not so,
Darker would be thy face, O brief today!
Earthward we'd bow beneath life's smiting woe,
Powerless to pray.
Something beyond! The immortal morning
stands
Above the night, clear shines her prescient brow;
The pendulous star in her transfigured hands
Lights up the Now.

MARY CLEMMER

WHEN YOU ARE OLD

When you are old and gray and full of sleep
And nodding by the fire, take down this book,
And slowly read, and dream of the soft look
You eyes had once, and of their shadows deep;

How many loved your moments of glad grace,
And loved your beauty with love false or true;
But one man loved the pilgrim soul in you,
And loved the sorrows of your changing face.

And bending down beside the glowing bars,
Murmur, a little sadly, how love fled
And paced upon the mountains overhead,
And hid his face amid a crowd of stars.

WILLIAM BUTLER YEATS

A MESSAGE

If there is any way, dear Lord
In which my heart may send her word
Of my continued love,
And of my joy in her relief
From pain—a joy not even grief
And loneliness may rise above,

Reveal it to me . . . for I long
To keep intact the tie so strong
Between us, from my birth,
That when we meet (as meet we must)
There shall be naught but perfect trust,
Such as we always knew on earth!

ANNA NELSON REED

IF HEARTS ARE DUST

And somewhere, far beyond the plane
Of earthly thought, beyond the sea
That bounds this life, they will meet thee,
And hold thee face to face again;
And when is done life's restless reign,
If I hereafter but regain
Heart's love, why should I troubled be
If hearts are dust?

By love's indissoluble chain
I know the grave does not retain
Heart's love; the very faith in me
Is pledge of an eternity,
Where I shall find heart's love again,
If hearts are dust.

JAMES TERRY WHITE

AT THE DAWN

As from my window at first glimpse of dawn
I watch the rising mist that heralds day,
And see by God's strong hand the curtain drawn
That through the night has hid the world away;
So I, through windows of my soul shall see
One day Death's fingers with resistless might
Draw back the curtained gloom that shadows life,
And on the darkness of Time's deepest night,
Let in the perfect Day—Eternity.

ALICE MACDONALD KIPLING

THE TESTING

When, in the dim beginning of the years,
God mixed in man the raptures and the tears,
And scattered through his brain the starry stuff,
He said, "Behold! Yet this is not enough,
For I must test his spirit to make sure
That he can dare the vision and endure.

"I will withdraw My face,
Veil Me in shadow for a certain space,
And leave behind only a broken clue,
A crevice where the glory glimmers through,
Some whisper from the sky,
Some footprint in the road to track Me by.

"I will leave man to make the fateful guess,
Will leave him torn between the no and yes,
Leave him unresting till he rests in Me,
Drawn upward by the choice that makes him free—
Leave him in tragic loneliness to choose,
With all in life to win or all to lose."

EDWIN MARKHAM

CROSSING THE BAR

Sunset and evening star,
And one clear call for me!
And may there be no moaning of the bar,
When I put out to sea,

But such a tide as moving seems asleep,
Too full for sound and foam,
When that which drew from out the boundless deep
Turns again home.

Twilight and evening bell,
And after that the dark!
And may there be no sadness of farewell,
When I embark;

For tho' from out our bourne of Time and Place
The flood may bear me far,
I hope to see my Pilot face to face
When I have crost the bar.

ALFRED TENNYSON

VI.

o never
star
was lost

FAITH

O never star
Was lost; here
We all aspire to heaven and there is heaven
Above us.
If I stoop
Into a dark tremendous sea of cloud,
It is but for a time; I press God's lamp
Close to my breast; its splendor soon or late
Will pierce the gloom. I shall emerge some day.

ROBERT BROWNING

LIFE

O Love triumphant over guilt and sin,
My Soul is soiled, but Thou shalt enter in;
My feet must stumble if I walk alone,
Lonely my heart, till beating by Thine own,
My will is weakness till it rest in Thine,
Cut off, I wither, thirsting for the Vine,
My deeds are dry leaves on a sapless tree,
My life is lifeless till it live in Thee!

FREDERICK LAWRENCE KNOWLES

DEPENDENCE ON GOD

Even as the needle, that directs the hour,
Touched with the loadstone, by the secret power
Of hidden nature, points unto the Pole;
Even so the wavering powers of my soul,
Touched by the virtue of Thy Spirit, flee
From what is earth, and point alone to Thee.

When I have faith to hold Thee by the hand,
I walk securely, and methinks I stand
More firm than Atlas; but when I forsake
The safe protection of Thine arm, I quake
Like wind-shaked reeds, and have no strength at all,
But like a vine, the prop cut down, I fall.

FRANCIS QUARLES

THE LORD IS MY SHEPHERD
PSALM 23

The Lord is my shepherd;
I shall not want.

He maketh me to lie down in green pastures:
he leadeth me beside the still waters.
He restoreth my soul:
he leadeth me in the paths of righteousness for
his name's sake.

Yea, though I walk through the valley of the
shadow of death,
I will fear no evil:
for thou art with me;
thy rod and thy staff they comfort me.

Thou preparest a table before me
in the presence of mine enemies:
thou anointest my head with oil;
my cup runneth over.
Surely goodness and mercy shall follow me all
the days of my life;
and I will dwell in the house of the Lord for ever.

KING JAMES VERSION

ON THE TWENTY-THIRD PSALM

In "pastures green"? Not always; sometimes He
Who knoweth best, in kindness leadeth me
In weary ways, where heavy shadows be.

And by "still waters"? No, not always so;
Oft times the heavy tempests round me blow,
And o'er my soul the waves and billows go.

But when the storm beats loudest, and I cry
Aloud for help, the Master standeth by,
And whispers to my soul, "Lo, it is I."

So, where he leads me, I can safely go,
And in the blest hereafter I shall know,
Why, in His wisdom, He hath led me so.

AUTHOR UNKNOWN

FOR ALL WHO NEED

For all who watch tonight—by land or sea or
air—
O Father, may they know that Thou art with
them there.

For all who weep tonight, the hearts that cannot
rest,
Reveal Thy love, that wondrous love which gave
for us Thy best.

For all who wake tonight, love's tender watch to
keep,
Watcher Divine, Thyself draw nigh, Thou who
dost never sleep.

For all who fear tonight, whate'er the dread
may be,
We ask for them the perfect peace of hearts that
rest in Thee.

Our own belov'd tonight, O Father, keep, and
where
Our love and succor cannot reach, now bless
them through our prayer.

And all who pray tonight, Thy wrestling hosts,
O Lord,
Make weakness strong, let them prevail
according to Thy word.

AUTHOR UNKNOWN

CLING TO FAITH

Cleave ever to the sunnier side of doubt,
And cling to faith beyond the forms of faith;
She reels not at the storm of warring words;
She brightens at the clash or "Yes" and "No";
She sees the best that glimmers through the
worst;
She feels the sun is hid but for the night;
She spies the summer through the winter bud;
She tastes the fruit before the blossom falls;
She hears the lark within the songless egg;
She finds the fountain where they wailed
"Mirage!"

ALFRED TENNYSON

LOST AND FOUND

I missed him when the sun began to bend;
I found him not when I had lost his rim;
With many tears I went in search of him,
Climbing high mountains which did still ascend
And gave me echoes when I called my friend;
Through cities vast and charnel-houses grim,
And high cathedrals where the light was dim,
Through books and arts and works without an
end,
But found him not—the friend whom I had lost.
And yet I found him—as I found the lark,
A sound in fields I heard but could not mark;
I found him nearest when I missed Him most;
I found him in my heart, a life in frost,
A light I knew not till my soul was dark.

GEORGE MAC DONALD

STILL, STILL WITH THEE

Still, still with Thee, when purple morning
breaketh,
When the bird waketh and the shadows flee;
Fairer than morning, lovelier than the daylight,
Dawns the sweet consciousness, I am with Thee!

Alone with Thee, amid the mystic shadows,
The solemn hush of nature newly born;
Alone with Thee, in breathless adoration,
In the calm dew and freshness of the morn.

Still, still with Thee, as to each new-born
morning
A fresh and solemn splendor still is given,
So doth this blessed consciousness awakening,
Breathe, each day, nearness unto Thee and
heaven.

When sinks the soul, subdued by toil, to
slumber,
Its closing eye looks up to Thee in prayer;
Sweet the repose beneath Thy wings o'ershading,
But sweeter still to wake and find Thee there.

So shall it be at last, in that bright morning
When the soul waketh and life's shadows flee;
Oh, in that hour fairer than daylight dawning,
Shall rise the glorious thought, I am with Thee!

HARRIET BEECHER STOWE

MY FAITH

This body is my house—it is not I:
Herein I sojourn till, in some far sky,
I lease a fairer dwelling, built to last
Till all the carpentry of time is past.
When from my high place viewing this lone star,
What shall I care where these poor timbers are?

What though the crumbling walls turn dust and
loam—
I shall have left them for a larger home!
What though the rafters break, the stanchions
rot,
When earth hath dwindled to a glimmering spot!
When thou, clay cottage, failest, I'll immerse
My long-cramped spirit in the universe.

Through uncomputed silences of space
I shall yearn upward to the leaning Face.
The ancient heavens will roll aside for me,
As Moses monarch's the dividing sea.
This body is my house—it is not I;
Triumphant in this faith I live, and die.

FREDERICK LAWRENCE KNOWLES

DESIGN

This is a piece too fair
To be the child of Chance, and not of Care.
No Atoms casually together hurl'd
Could e'er produce so beautiful a world.

JOHN DRYDEN

THERE IS NO UNBELIEF

There is no unbelief;
Whoever plants a seed beneath the sod
And waits to see it push away the clod—
He trusts in God.

There is no unbelief;
Whoever says beneath the sky,
"Be patient, heart; light breaketh by and by,"
Trusts the Most High.

There is no unbelief;
Whoever sees 'neath winter's field of snow,
The silent harvest of the future grow—
God's power must know.

There is no unbelief;
Whoever lies down on his couch to sleep.
Content to lock each sense in slumber deep,
Knows God will keep.

There is no unbelief;
Whoever says "tomorrow," "the unknown,"
"The future," trusts that power alone
He dares disown.

There is no unbelief;
The heart that looks on when the eyelids
close,
And dares to live when life has only woes.
God's comfort knows.

There is no unbelief;
For this by day and night unconsciously
The heart lives by the faith the lips deny,
God knoweth why.

ELIZABETH YORK CASE

GOD OF THE EARTH, THE SKY, THE SEA

God of the earth, the sky, the sea,
Maker of all above, below,
Creation lives and moves in Thee;
Thy present life through all doth flow.

Thy love is in the sun-shine's glow,
Thy life is in the quickening air;
When lightnings flash and storm winds blow
There is Thy power, Thy law is there.

We feel Thy calm at evening's hour,
They grandeur in the march of night,
And when the morning breaks in power,
We hear Thy word, "Let there be light."

But higher far, and far more clear,
Thee in man's spirit we behold,
Thine image and Thyself are there,—
Th' in-dwelling, proclaimed of old.

SAMUEL LONGFELLOW

WE LIVE BY FAITH

We live by faith; but faith is not the slave
Of text and legend.   Reason's voice and God's;
Nature's and Duty's, never are at odds.
What asks our Father of His children, save
Justice, mercy and humility,
A reasonable service of good deeds,
Pure living, tenderness to human needs,
Reverence and trust, and prayer for light to see
The Master's footprints in our daily ways.

JOHN GREENLEAF WHITTIER

ALL THINGS BRIGHT
AND BEAUTIFUL

All things bright and beautiful,
All creatures great and small,
All things wise and wonderful,
The Lord God made them all.

Each little flower that opens,
Each little bird that sings,
He made their glowing colours,
He made their tiny wings.

The purple-headed mountain,
The river running by,
The sunset, and the morning
That brightens up the sky,

The cold wind in the winter,
The pleasant summer sun,
The ripe fruits in the garden,
He made them every one.

The tall trees in the greenwood,
The meadows where we play,
The rushes by the water,
We gather every day.

He gave us eyes to see them,
And lips that we might tell
How great is God Almighty,
Who has made all things well.

CECIL FRANCIS ALEXANDER

WINGS

Be like the bird
That, pausing in her flight
Awhile on boughs too slight,
Feels them give way
Beneath her and yet sings,
Knowing that she hath wings.

VICTOR HUGO

THE UNDYING SOUL

Yet howsoever changed or tost,
Not even a wreath of mist is lost,
No atom can itself exhaust.

So shall the soul's superior force
Live on and run its endless course
In God's unlimited universe.

JOHN GREENLEAF WHITTIER

PRAYER

I asked for bread; God gave a stone instead.
Yet, while I pillowed there my weary head,
The angels made a ladder of my dreams,
Which upward to celestial mountains led.
And when I woke beneath the morning's beams,
Around my resting place fresh manna lay;
And, praising God, I went upon my way.
For I was fed.

God answers prayer; sometimes, when hearts are
weak,
He gives the very gifts believers seek.
But often faith must learn a deeper rest,
And trust God's silence when He does not speak;
For He whose name is Love will send the best.
Stars may burn out, nor mountain walls endure,
But God is true, His promises are sure
For those who seek.

AUTHOR UNKNOWN

THREE WORDS OF STRENGTH

There are three lessons I would write,
Three words, as with a burning pen,
In tracings of eternal light,
Upon the hearts of men.

Have Hope. Though clouds environ round,
And gladness hides her face in scorn,
Put off the shadow from thy brow:
No night but hath its morn.

Have Faith. Where'er thy bark is driven—
The calm's disport, the tempest's mirth—
Know this: God rules the hosts of heaven,
The inhabitants of earth.

Have Love. Not love alone for one,
But man, as man, thy brother call;
And scatter, like a circling sun,
Thy charities on all.

FRIEDRICH VON SCHILLER